W9-AYB-558

DATE DUE		

13442

**973.4
NEL**

Nelson, Sheila.

**Thomas Jefferson's
America : the
Louisiana Purchase
1800-1811**

THOMAS JEFFERSON'S AMERICA

The Louisiana Purchase 1800~1811

TITLE LIST

THOMAS JEFFERSON'S AMERICA:
The Louisiana Purchase 1800-1811

BY
SHEILA NELSON

MASON CREST PUBLISHERS
PHILADELPHIA

THOMAS JEFFERSON'S AMERICA

Mason Crest Publishers Inc.
370 Reed Road
Broomall, Pennsylvania 19008
(866) MCP-BOOK (toll free)

First printing
1 2 3 4 5 6 7 8 9 10

Library of Congress Cataloging-in-Publication Data

Nelson, Sheila.
  Thomas Jefferson's America : the Louisiana Purchase (1800–1811) / by Sheila Nelson.
      p. cm. — (How America became America)
  Includes bibliographical references and index.
  ISBN 1-59084-904-3   ISBN 1-59084-900-0 (series)
  1. Louisiana Purchase—Juvenile literature. 2. United States—History—1797–1801—Juvenile literature. 3.
United States—History—1801–1809—Juvenile literature. 4. Jefferson, Thomas, 1743–1826—Juvenile litera-
ture. 5. United States—Territorial expansion—Juvenile literature. I. Title. II. Series.
  E333.N45 2005
  973.4'6—dc22
                                    2004013692

Design by M.K. Bassett-Harvey.
Produced by Harding House Publishing Service, Inc.
Cover design by Dianne Hodack.
Printed in the Hashemite Kingdom of Jordan.

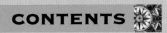

CONTENTS

INTRODUCTION

by Dr. Jack Rakove

Today's America is not the same geographical shape as the first American colonies—and the concept of America has evolved as well over the years.

When the thirteen original states declared their independence from Great Britain, most Americans still lived within one or two hours modern driving time from the Atlantic coast. In other words, the Continental Congress that approved the Declaration of Independence on July 4, 1776, was continental in name only. Yet American leaders like George Washington, Benjamin Franklin, and Thomas Jefferson also believed that the new nation did have a continental destiny. They expected it to stretch at least as far west as the Mississippi River, and they imagined that it could extend even further. The framers of the Federal Constitution of 1787 provided that western territories would join the Union on equal terms with the original states. In 1803, President Jefferson brought that continental vision closer to reality by purchasing the vast Louisiana Territory from France. In the 1840s, negotiations with Britain and a war with Mexico brought the United States to the Pacific Ocean.

This expansion created great opportunities, but it also brought serious costs. As Americans surged westward, they created a new economy of family farms and large plantations. But between the Ohio River and the Gulf of Mexico, expansion also brought the continued growth of plantation slavery for millions of African Americans. Political struggle over the extension of slavery west of the Mississippi was one of the major causes of the Civil War that killed hundreds of thousands of Americans in the 1860s but ended with the destruction of slavery. Creating opportunities for American farmers also meant displacing Native Americans from the lands their ancestors had occupied for centuries. The opening of the west encouraged massive immigration not only from Europe but also from Asia, as Chinese workers came to labor in the California Gold Rush and the building of the railroads.

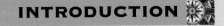

By the end of the nineteenth century, Americans knew that their great age of territorial expansion was over. But immigration and the growth of modern industrial cities continued to change the American landscape. Now Americans moved back and forth across the continent in search of economic opportunities. African Americans left the South in massive numbers and settled in dense concentrations in the cities of the North. The United States remained a magnet for immigration, but new immigrants came increasingly from Mexico, Central America, and Asia.

Ever since the seventeenth century, expansion and migration across this vast landscape have shaped American history. These books are designed to explain how this process has worked. They tell the story of how modern America became the nation it is today.

Thomas Jefferson

One
JEFFERSON'S CONCEPT OF AMERICA

When Thomas Jefferson was a twenty-two-year-old law student in Williamsburg, Virginia, he stood in the doorway of the House of Burgesses and listened to the young legislator Patrick Henry rail against the Stamp Act. Britain had passed the act, taxing all legal documents as a way to increase their income from the colonies, and the colonists were outraged.

"Caesar had his Brutus," Patrick Henry thundered, "Charles the First his Cromwell, and George the Third—" He paused and men all throughout the closely packed House shouted "Treason!" Brutus had helped murder Caesar. Cromwell had defeated Charles the First and had him executed. George the Third now ruled Britain and the American colonies; any talk of his downfall was *treasonous*. Henry did not hesitate, but finished his sentence, "George the Third—may profit by their example. If this be treason, make the most of it."

Treasonous means having the characteristic of attempting to overthrow the government.

Standing at the back of the crowd, Thomas Jefferson listened to Henry's fiery speech and must have felt a thrill run through him. This was his first taste of revolution. Over the next ten years, he and other politicians would grow increasingly dissatisfied with the restrictions Britain imposed on them, until they finally declared their independence and fought the war that would free them to govern themselves.

"We hold these truths to be self-evident," Thomas Jefferson wrote in the Declaration of Independence, "that all men are created equal, that they are endowed by their Creator with certain unalienable Rights, that among these are Life, Liberty, and the pursuit of Happiness."

The Founding Fathers agreed on these "unalienable Rights," and at first, that was enough. As the country began to grow and develop, however, they began to disagree about how these rights should be granted. Two groups developed—the Federalists and the Democratic-Republicans. At first, these were not political parties as we think of them today. They were simply terms used to categorize men who thought differently about the government's place in their new country. No political parties existed during the first years after the Revolutionary War, since the founders of the United States believed such parties would divide the country and make it weaker. As time went on, though, such differences did evolve into political parties.

Federal *means the central authority of government.*

A **dictatorship** *is a form of government in which one person has power.*

Proponents *are people who are in favor of something.*

To **deport** *means to send a noncitizen back to the country from where he came.*

Patrick Henry

The Federalists were men like George Washington and Alexander Hamilton. They believed the **federal** government should have a strong, central role in governing the country. They wanted to establish a national bank and to build up a strong army and navy to protect the country. Many of the northern businessmen and manufacturers were Federalists.

The Democratic-Republicans, on the other hand, were in favor of states' rights. They were suspicious of giving a central government too much power because they were afraid it could turn into a **dictatorship**. They believed that by giving the individual states most of the governing power, a system would be set up that would keep any part of the government from becoming too powerful.

By the end of George Washington's first term as President, the two groups had developed into two distinct political parties. Despite the fears of the nation's founders that political parties would lead to division, the rival groups actually led to a stronger government. The existence of more than one political party added to the system of balancing power, each serving to keep the other in line.

Thomas Jefferson was one of the main **proponents** of the Democratic-Republicans. In fact, his influence was so great the party was sometimes called the Jeffersonian Republicans. Jefferson had been involved in the shaping of the United States from the beginning. He had written the Declaration of Independence and served as secretary of state for George Washington.

Jefferson had definite ideas about the values and ideals he thought the new country should work toward. He wanted the United States to become a country of small family farms. He be-

George Washington

lieved farming life was superior to any other way of living, and he especially disliked cities and industries.

In the 1796 election, Jefferson ran for President against John Adams. Adams was a Federalist and had been George Washington's Vice President. Although they were running for different parties, the Constitution did not account for more than one political party and when Jefferson came in second, he became Adams's Vice President.

While John Adams was President, Congress passed the Alien and Sedition Acts. The Alien Act allowed the President to *deport* any foreigners he thought might be dangerous and raised the residency requirement for American citizenship from five to fourteen years. The Sedition Act made it a crime to publish false and negative reports about the President and the government.

The Federalists hoped the Alien and Sedition Acts would build up their party. Most of the Federalist supporters were wealthy Northern merchants, while the poor immigrants who flocked to the United States from Europe tended to join with Thomas Jefferson and the Democratic-Republicans. Raising the number of years it took to become a citizen would limit

Political parties encouraged the growth of newspapers. The
National Gazette *supported the Democratic-Republicans.*

the number of new voters joining the Democratic-Republicans.

Neither the Federalists nor the Democratic-Republicans really believed the common people were capable of governing themselves. The Federalists thought the wealthy and educated upper classes should make the decisions on behalf of the people. Thomas Jefferson and the Democratic-Republicans believed the people could be educated and taught to make wise gov-

John Adams

This political cartoon portrays Jefferson, supported by Thomas Paine, the French philosophers, and Satan, about to fling the Constitution into the fire.

To **repeal** means to annul by an authoritative act.

Inaugurated means sworn into office.

Aaron Burr

erning choices for themselves. Jefferson's party welcomed the poor and oppressed immigrants and gave them hope of becoming a part of their new country and having a voice in the political decisions that affected their lives.

The Alien and Sedition Acts infuriated the Democratic-Republicans. Thomas Jefferson wrote the Kentucky Resolutions, which were passed in the Kentucky legislature four months after the Alien and Sedition Acts went into effect, while James Madison wrote a set of similar resolutions for the Virginia legislature. The Kentucky Resolutions claimed the federal government had over-stepped their bounds by passing the Alien and Sedition Acts. The acts violated the First Amendment rights of freedom of speech and freedom of the press, and the federal government had passed laws going beyond its authority. The states should refuse to accept the acts, stated the Kentucky Resolutions.

The Federalist Party passed the Alien and Sedition Acts because it was trying to win support for itself. Its members thought the acts would make it harder for their rivals, the Democratic-Republicans, to build a strong party and would keep people from saying negative things about their party. Instead, the people were so angered by the acts that many left the Federalists and turned to the Democratic-Republican Party.

The unpopular Alien and Sedition Acts were the beginning of the end for the Federalist Party. Adams and Jefferson ran against each other in the presidential election of 1800, as they had in 1796, but this time Jefferson won. His Vice President was Aaron Burr. One of Jefferson's early actions as President was to **repeal** the Alien and Sedition Acts.

Thomas Jefferson the Inventor

Besides being President of the United States, Thomas Jefferson was an avid inventor. Many of his inventions and improvements were used at his home in Monticello.

Among his inventions, Jefferson designed a plow and an improved dumbwaiter. He invented the swivel chair and a book stand, which could hold five books, that collapsed to form a box. Jefferson designed a mechanism for double doors so that both would move when one was opened or closed. He also perfected a portable copying press for use in his foreign travels.

Jefferson's foreign travels introduced him to foods that he brought back to America. He developed a fondness for pasta dishes, and when Jefferson returned to America, he invented a macaroni-making machine. And, he brought the recipe for vanilla ice cream to America from France.

Thomas Jefferson was ***inaugurated*** as President on March 4, 1801. At the time, he was staying in a boarding house near the Senate. On a bright, sunny day, Jefferson walked to his inauguration with several of his fellow boarders. He was sworn in as President, gave his inaugural speech in a voice so quiet most of the people in the room could not hear him, and then walked back to the boarding house. Eating supper that night with the other boarders, he sat at the table as usual. The men laughed and talked just as

Thomas Jefferson's fivesided bookstand

17

they always did. A visitor from Baltimore was the only person to even mention the inauguration. Sitting next to Jefferson, the visitor leaned over and congratulated him. Jefferson smiled and suggested the man wait until he had been President a year before deciding whether or not he should be congratulated.

Jefferson started his time as President simply, as an ordinary man. His ideals for the country reflected this simplicity. He pictured little farms dotting the countryside, each one owned by a different family. He believed the act of farming would make people better, and the farms would make the country a better place.

According to Jefferson, agriculture, especially the growing of food crops, taught people self-sufficiency.

Jefferson believed that ideally, America's *agrarian* society would consist of many smaller, independent farms rather than large plantations. The large plantations that existed in the Southern states generally grew mainly one crop each—usually cotton or tobacco—instead of a variety of food crops. This made the plantations very dependent on merchants for their food, as well as for loans to purchase more land and slaves to work the fields. Small family farms were independent, as Jefferson envi-

The Capitol in 1800

18

sioned, but they were also poor. Most people were not willing to give up their wealth for the opportunity of being completely self-sufficient.

Part of Jefferson's vision for this ideal America included educating the people so they could take part in governing themselves. He thought most Americans did not understand enough to make

Agrarian *means relating to farms and farmers, agriculture.*

The President Who Almost Wasn't

Thomas Jefferson and Aaron Burr were the candidates in the 1800 presidential election. Each member of the Electoral College had two votes to cast for President. Republicans had arranged for several electors to split their votes so Burr would come in second. Each elector thought someone else was going to do so, causing the election to end in a tie. The election was sent to the House of Representatives to be resolved. Jefferson won by one vote.

Representative William C. C. Claiborne cast the deciding vote. It was later discovered that Claiborne had been elected to the House before he had reached the constitutional age limit, making his election illegal.

20

Thomas Jefferson believed in equality for all. To express this belief, he ordered a round table constructed so each person at his table would feel of equal importance when seated at dinner. He also instigated the "handshake" to replace the customary British tradition of bowing, as shaking hands seemed to him a gesture more symbolic of equality.

smart choices, but he believed they could be taught to make good decisions. After Jefferson retired from politics in 1809, he founded the University of Virginia. The university accepted both students well off enough to pay the tuition and poor students who were intelligent but could not afford to pay.

One problem with Jefferson's agrarian ideal was that if people were going to succeed at farming, they would have no time

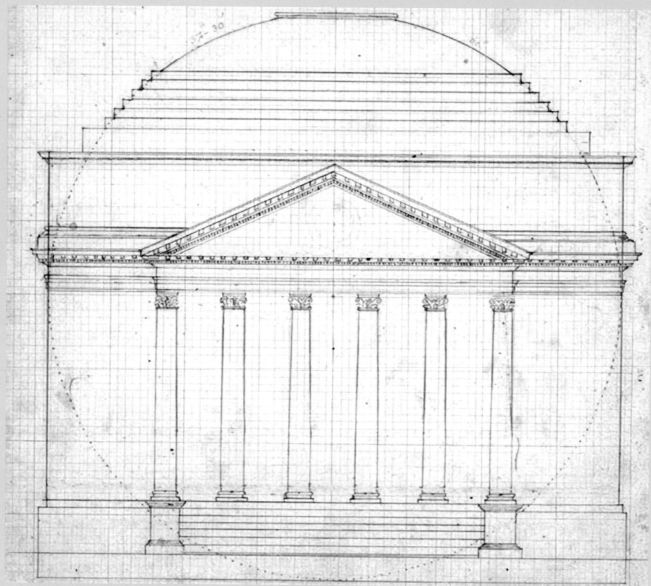

Jefferson's sketch of the University of Virginia's rotunda

left over to get involved with the governing of the country. Having black slaves do most of the hard and tedious labor of farming would solve this problem. Here, Jefferson's ideals conflicted with each other. Slaves would give farmers the time they needed to educate themselves and participate in running the country, but Jefferson thought slavery was a "moral and political *depravity.*"

Depravity *means the quality of being evil or corrupt.*

Jefferson believed that enslaving people was evil. Despite this, he was not sure how to solve the problem. Slavery was such a big part of the Southern way of life that he believed it would take time to end it completely. Also, he was afraid if the slaves were freed quickly, and immediately given equal rights, they would take revenge on their former masters.

To keep this from happening, Jefferson thought the best thing would be to free the slaves gradually. He thought the freed slaves

The original plan for the University of Virginia

Peers *are those of the same social standing, usually based on age, grade, or status.*

Liberal *means being open-minded, or not strict in observing traditional ways or thoughts.*

Jefferson admired Native Americans

should be settled in their own country on the coast of Africa, where the United States would help them financially until they were established.

Like most white people of his time, Jefferson thought the black slaves were inferior to white people. Unlike many of his **peers**, however, Jefferson thought this inferiority was probably not because the black people were naturally less intelligent, but because they had been enslaved and oppressed. He wrote that blacks were equal to whites in memory and in bravery, and that they were generally more gifted musically than whites. He thought if the black slaves were freed and given the same educational opportunities as white people, they would likely turn out to be intellectually equal as well. In today's world, we would consider Jefferson to be prejudiced against African Americans, but it is very hard to think thoughts that are different from everyone else around you; Jefferson's thoughts were extremely **liberal** for his time.

White Americans of Thomas Jefferson's time usually considered Native Americans inferior as well. Jefferson, however, deeply admired American Indians and the Indian culture. He believed the Indians should become citizens of the United States, with rights equal to those of white people.

The ideals Jefferson had for the United States included his views on the way the government should interact with the religious beliefs of Americans. The famous phrase "the separation of church and state" comes from a letter Jefferson wrote to the Danbury Baptist Association while he was President. The association had first written to Jefferson concerned about religious freedoms. England and many European countries had one national church.

Slave sale in Easton, Maryland

The government supported this church, and people belonging to other churches often faced persecution. Many immigrants to the United States had left Europe to escape religious oppression. The people were worried the U.S. gov-ernment, or the state governments, might begin to favor certain churches over others.

Jefferson assured the Baptist Association "that religion is a matter which lies solely be-tween man and his God, that he owes account

25

Thomas Jefferson's Epitaph

Jefferson wrote his own epitaph to be inscribed on his tomb. He wanted it to mention what he had done for the American people and not what they had done for him. His presidency was not mentioned.

Here was Buried Thomas Jefferson

Author of the Declaration of American Independence

Of The Statute of Virginia for Religious Freedom

And Father of The University Of Virginia

Born April 2. 1743. O.S. [Old Style]

Died July 4. 1826

to none other for his faith or his worship, . . . that their legislature should make no law respecting an establishment of religion, or prohibiting the free exercise thereof, thus building a wall of separation between Church and State." He wanted to make sure the Baptists knew the U.S. government would not interfere with their church.

Jefferson's words to the Baptists were an echo of the Constitution's First Amendment— "Congress shall make no law respecting an establishment of religion, or prohibiting the free exercise thereof." The amendment was not in- tended to protect the government from too much church influence, so much as to protect the churches from too much government influence.

Three years after he wrote the Declaration of Independence, Jefferson drafted the Virginia Act for Establishing Religious Freedom. This act declared it was the natural right of all men to be free to hold their own religious opinions and not to be forced to support or attend any particular church. Six years later, and after much debate, the Virginia legislature finally made the act law.

At the end of his life, the three accomplishments of which Jefferson was proudest were the Declaration of Independence, the Virginia Act for Establishing Religious Freedom, and the founding of the University of Virginia. These three achievements reflected his highest *ideals*: independence, religious freedom, and education for all.

Ideals *are standards of perfection.*

Jefferson's grave

What Does O.S. Mean on Jefferson's Tombstone?

O.S. means Old Style. The Old Style calendar was in use in England and the colonies until 1752, when the English adopted the Gregorian (New Style) calendar, which we still use today. When the new calendar was adopted, eleven days were added to the current date to bring the calendar date up to match the astronomical calendar. This means that, although Thomas Jefferson was born on April 2, his birthday is celebrated April 13, to reflect the Gregorian calendar.

Two
THE REALITY OF JEFFERSONIAN AMERICA

Monticello, Thomas Jefferson's elegant home, stands on a hilltop near Charlottesville, Virginia. Jefferson designed the house himself and laid out the plantation farms on his five thousand acres. When he was at home, he would ride out to inspect the shops and farms on his land. "From breakfast, or noon at the latest, to dinner, I am mostly on horseback," he wrote, "Attending to My Farm or other concerns, which I find healthful to my body, mind, and affairs."

After reading Jefferson's fervent condemnations of slavery, you might think he himself owned no slaves. In fact, however, nearly 150 slaves lived and worked on Jefferson's Monticello plantation. These slaves worked the outlying farms and served around the Monticello home.

Many people, reading how Jefferson claimed to hate slavery, wonder why he did not just free his own slaves. Unfortunately, life was not that simple, at least not from Jefferson's perspective. Both financial and moral reasons interfered with any plans he might have had for freeing his slaves.

Jefferson was born into life as a slaveholder. He had inherited most of his slaves when his father died. Almost all of his wealth was tied up in his land and slaves. During his lifetime, Jefferson accumulated tens of thousands of dollars of debt. He loved expensive foods and wines and lavished money on his beloved Monticello

Collateral *is something placed as security pledged by a borrower to ensure payment of a debt.*

Emancipation *means the act of making free.*

and its farms. As his possessions, Jefferson's slaves served as **collateral** on his debts. Legal restrictions involved with these debts preventing him from freeing them.

Morally, Jefferson worried that suddenly freeing all the slaves would be the same as deserting them. They would have to struggle for survival against difficulties they had never faced. "As far as I can judge from the experiments which have been made," he wrote to a friend, "to give liberty to, or rather to abandon persons whose habits have been formed in slavery is like abandoning children." This fear conflicted with his deeply felt belief that slavery was wrong and should be abolished. To overcome both these problems, Jefferson developed the idea of gradual **emancipation**. Slavery would be phased out slowly, making sure the freed slaves were educated and prepared to live independent lives. This idea was never carried out, however, though Jefferson may have eased his guilt by promising himself that one day he would get around to making it happen.

Monticello, Jefferson's home

Monticello

Thomas Jefferson's home, Monticello, was one of his pride and joys. It is the only home in America that is on the United Nations' World Heritage List of sites to be protected.

The design and construction of the home began in 1769, and was completed when he left for Europe in 1784. Jefferson designed the enlargement of the house in 1796; remodeling was completed in 1809.

Monticello has forty-three rooms—thirty-three in the house, four in the pavilions, and six under the south terrace. Much of the material used in the house was from Jefferson's land. The bricks and nails were made at Monticello, and the timber came from Jefferson's property. Slaves completed much of the home's woodworking.

Thomas Jefferson's family had to sell the property after his death to settle his debts. It was eventually sold to the Thomas Jefferson Memorial Foundation, which administers the historic site.

Africans brought to America endured terrible conditions.

The society in which Jefferson lived all his life accepted slavery. It took for granted that slaves were necessary to work the large plantations of the South. Thomas Jefferson was a Southern gentleman, and his way of life required slave labor to maintain. No matter how much he wrote about the evils of slavery, he must have found it difficult to walk away from his luxurious lifestyle and become a small, **subsistence farmer**.

Thomas Jefferson was an **idealist**. If people had enough education, he thought, they would usually make good decisions. In his mind, he saw a nation of little farms, families nourishing the soil and being nourished by it in return. Slavery had been abolished in

*A **subsistence farmer** is one who produces what the family needs to survive, with very little left to sell.*

*An **idealist** is someone who is guided by his standards of perfection.*

The Sally Hemings Controversy

During Thomas Jefferson's first term as President, a newspaper in Richmond, Virginia, wrote a story accusing Jefferson of fathering several children by one of his slaves, Sally Hemings. Sally served as a lady's maid for Jefferson's daughters. She was very pretty, with long, straight hair.

Since the story first appeared in 1802, the controversy has been ongoing. Even today, historians still debate whether or not Jefferson really was the father of Sally's children.

In 1998, DNA tests confirmed descendants of these children had Jefferson DNA. The controversy was not resolved, however. Some people claimed the tests proved conclusively that Jefferson had fathered Sally's children, while others argued that one of Jefferson's relatives could just as easily have been the father.

Native American chief with headdress

Jefferson's dream, and, because he was not sure what else should be done with them, the former slaves would be settled in their own colony on the coast of Africa. The Indians—the "noble savages"—would live among the American people. As the Native culture was absorbed and mingled with that of the white Americans, a new and stronger culture would be created in the United States. People would worship God as they chose, without fear the government would make laws restricting that right.

Jefferson's vision for America was defeated by reality. Regardless of how much education people have, differences of opinion always exist. Just because a person had a lot of education did not mean he would agree with Jefferson. Educated people rarely chose to live on little farms. Freed slaves were not always excited about moving to Africa, where many of them had never been. Native Americans wanted to preserve their own way of life rather than be absorbed by white culture. And Jefferson himself often did not act according to his written ideals.

The wide gap between the ideals Jefferson wrote about and the reality of life in America makes him look like a very inconsistent person. He said people should live on small family farms, but he lived on a five-thousand-acre plantation. He claimed slavery was evil, but he owned over a hundred slaves. He revered the Indians, but he maneuvered them into selling off their ancestral land, forcing them into smaller and smaller areas.

Jefferson's life had many inconsistencies. He had many ideas about what would make the country a better place, but if the ideas were not working out, he modified them or abandoned them. Besides being an idealist, Jefferson was also a *pragmatist*.

Some historians think Jefferson had several chances to help abolish slavery and work toward creating a country of small family farms—but he ignored these opportunities. For example, Jefferson wrote that while he was a member of the Virginia legislature, he suggested children born to slaves after 1800 should be declared free; no real evidence indicates he tried to make the suggestion a reality.

When Kentucky became a state, Jefferson missed another opportunity. Kentucky's location between slave and free states created *controversy* about which the new state would become. Some historians argue that if Jefferson had spoken out in favor of Kentucky becoming a free state, he would have had enough influence to make it happen.

The vast tract of land acquired in the Louisiana Purchase was another missed chance. Many northerners fought to keep slavery from spreading west into the new territories. Jefferson, however, allowed and even encouraged the expansion of slavery to the West.

Some historians think the main reason Thomas Jefferson did not try very hard to make his ideals a reality was that he was afraid his fellow plantation owners would stop liking him. Jefferson was a well-respected man in the United States, and he enjoyed the

*A **pragmatist** is someone who has a practical approach to problems.*

***Controversy** is a discussion marked by opposing views.*

Thomas Jefferson

Pestilential means causing something that would lead to the destruction of life.

Industrialists are people who are engaged in manufacturing.

$20 REWARD.

Ranaway from the Subscriber, on the 22nd December last, his negro man MARTIN, aged about 23 years. He has a pleasing countenance, round face, is quick spoken, and can tell a very plausible story ; he is a shining black, stout built, with large limbs, short fingers, and small feet; the toe next to his great toe has been mashed off.

The above reward will be paid on his delivery to me, or at any Jail in North Carolina.

JAMES R. WOOD.
Wadesboro', Feb. 5, 1844.

Advertisement for a runaway slave

approval of his peers, men of similar education and social standing. If Jefferson had seriously attempted to end slavery, he would have made himself very unpopular with Southern landowners.

Ending slavery would change the face of the South. The huge Southern plantations could not exist without slave labor. Without slaves, Southerners would turn from farming to other industries. Cities would spring up. Jefferson hated cities. The cities of Europe overflowed with disease and corruption, and Jefferson cringed at the thought of such miserable places obliterating his cherished farmlands. "I view great cities as *pestilential* to the morals, the health and the liberties of man," he wrote to a friend.

However, industry and the cities that grew up around it played a great part in the financial success of the Northern states. Businesses in the North injected American culture with variety and energy. The South, relying mostly on its vast fields of cotton and tobacco for income, locked itself into dependencies on Europe and the northern half of the country. But the Southern agrarian culture was—apart from its need for slaves—the closest America ever came to Jefferson's ideal.

As new territories in the West opened up, Jefferson found his hatred of cities was stronger than his hatred of slavery. He could not bear to see the beautiful wilderness land overrun by *industrialists*. Instead, he encouraged farmers, including many slave owners, to spread out into the West.

To the slaves, being sent further south or west was devastating. Freedom was suddenly hundreds of miles farther away. Families were separated from each other by distances too great to have hope of ever being reunited.

Jefferson, however, thought the spread of slavery to the West might be a good thing. In fact, he thought allowing slavery to spread out could be the way to gradually bring freedom to the slaves. In a letter, he wrote:

> All know that permitting the slaves of the South to spread into the West will not add one being to that unfortunate condition, that it will increase the happiness of those existing, and by spreading them over a larger surface, will dilute the evil everywhere and facilitate the means of getting finally rid of it, an event more anxiously wished by those on whom it presses than by the noisy pretenders to exclusive humanity.

Slave cabins

A Southern plantation house

Jefferson viewed the National Bridge in western Virginia as the symbolic gateway to the West.

Jefferson's belief that slavery was wrong had not changed. Making sure an agrarian way of life prevailed in the new Western territories, however, meant allowing the expansion of slavery.

Americans Indians also found themselves affected by the gap between Jefferson's ideals and reality. Jefferson admired the Indians a great deal. Their culture fascinated him, and he thought of them as "noble savages." He believed the best solution to the ongoing Indian conflicts was for the Indians to adopt the lifestyle of the white Americans. In a speech to a group of Native American tribes, he said:

> You will unite yourselves with us, join in our great councils and form one people with us and we shall all be Americans. You will mix with us by marriage. Your blood will run in our veins and will spread with us over this great island.

Jefferson saw that the spread of the white man across North America did not leave any room for the traditional Native American culture. Since he admired the Indians, however, he encouraged them to intermarry with the white settlers and to join the United States. They would be equal but ***indistinguishable*** from white people.

Indistinguishable means unable to tell apart from anyone or anything else.

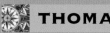

Most Native Americans did not want to lose their traditional way of life. Unable to absorb them, Jefferson and other American leaders now faced the issue of how to live side by side with a culture so different from their own. The United States was expanding quickly, taking more and more land for plantation farms and building towns on the ancestral lands of the Indians. The Native tribes were being crowded out.

The Louisiana Purchase, adding hundreds of thousands of square miles to the country, inspired Jefferson to move the Indians west. After Jefferson's death, reservations would be set up for Indian tribes in the West. Ignoring the unhappy western Indians, eastern tribes would be forcibly uprooted and marched west for hundreds of miles to the reservations of Oklahoma Territory.

In Jefferson's time, things had not yet reached this point. To deal with Indian tribes who did not want to leave their homes, Jefferson spoke to the Indians, encouraging them to settle west of the Mississippi River and become farmers. Privately, he wrote to William Henry Harrison, the governor of the Indiana Territory, telling him how to pressure reluctant tribes into selling their lands and moving west:

> To promote this disposition to exchange lands which they have to spare and we want for necessaries . . . we shall push our trading houses, and be glad to see the good and influential individuals among them run in debt, because we observe that when these debts get beyond

Jefferson's Address to the Choctaw Nation

On December 17, 1803, President Jefferson spoke to a group of Choctaw Indians who were visiting Washington. At that time, the tribe lived in what is now Mississippi.

We have long heard of your nation as a numerous, peaceable, and friendly people; but this is the first visit we have had from its great men at the seat of our government. I welcome you here; am glad to take you by the hand, and to assure you, for your nation, that we are their friends. Born in the same land, we ought to live as brothers, doing to each other all the good we can, and not listening to wicked men, who may endeavor to make us enemies. By living in peace, we can help and prosper one another; by waging war, we can kill and destroy many on both sides; but those who survive will not be the happier for that. Then, brothers, let it forever be peace and good neighborhood between us. Our seventeen States compose a great and growing nation. Their children are as the leaves of the trees, which the winds are spreading over the forest. But we are just also. We take from no nation what belongs to it. Our growing numbers make us always willing to buy lands from our red brethren, when they are willing to sell. But be assured we never mean to disturb them in their possessions. On the contrary, the lines established between us by mutual consent, shall be sacredly preserved, and will protect your lands from all encroachments by our own people or any others. We will give you a copy of the law, made by our great Council, for punishing our people, who may encroach on your lands, or injure you otherwise. Carry it with you to your homes, and preserve it, as the shield which we spread over you, to protect your land, your property and persons.

Chippewa head chief

Cession *means yielding to another.*

Circumscribe *means to constrict the range.*

Visionary *means having foresight and imagination.*

what the individuals can pay, they become willing to lop them off by a ***cession*** of lands. . . . In this way our settlements will gradually ***circumscribe*** and approach the Indians, and they will in time either incorporate with us as citizens of the United States or remove beyond the Missisip[p]i.

Thomas Jefferson's life was a blend of the ***visionary*** ideals of his writings and the blunt, sometimes harsh, pragmatism of his actions. He wanted both the black slaves and the Indians to live free and independent lives. The culture of America at this time, however, did not make this easy. At the end of his life, Jefferson wrote that the slavery issue must be resolved by another generation. That resolution would come in the form of the Civil War, the bloodiest war the United States had ever fought.

A
Map of
LEWIS AND CLARK'S TRACK,
Across the Western Portion of
North America
From the
MISSISSIPPI TO THE PACIFIC OCEAN;
By Order of the Executive
of the
UNITED STATES.

Three

THE ROAD TO THE LOUISIANA PURCHASE

Napoleon Bonaparte, Emperor of France, loved baths. He would stay in the bathtub for nearly an hour every morning, reading the newspaper, conducting business, and adding more hot water every few minutes.

Early on the morning of April 7, 1803, the Emperor was relaxing in his bathtub when his brothers Joseph and Lucien came to see him. Napoleon leaned back in the tub and chatted with his brothers until they finally gathered their courage and brought up the real reason for their visit: Was Napoleon really thinking of selling Louisiana to the Americans?

Joseph and Lucien were horrified their brother would even consider getting rid of the North American territory. Forty years earlier, Louisiana had belonged to France, but the king—who thought the land was a worthless stretch of swamps and wilderness—had gotten rid of it by presenting it to Spain as a gift. The French people did not agree with their king's de-cision, and ever since, they had been trying to get it back. Only a few years earlier, Napoleon had negotiated a secret treaty with Spain to re-gain possession of Louisiana. French troops had not even officially taken over New Orleans yet. The French people had been overjoyed to have Louisiana back. They would not happily part with it again so quickly.

Parliament *is a body of government.*

Guerrilla-style *means fought in an irregular manner, such as independent units carrying out harassment and sabotage.*

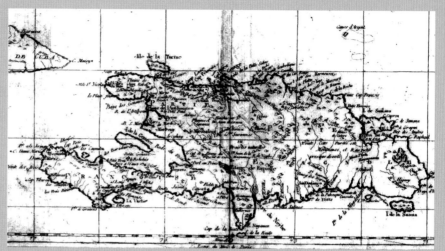

Map of St. Dominque

Pierre Touissant L'Overture led the rebellion against France in St. Domingue.

"I will expose your plan to the **parliament**," Joseph threatened. "They will never agree to it."

Angrily, Joseph and Lucien started to leave the room. Napoleon stood up in his bath and yelled after them, "I do not need anyone's permission!"

The brothers came back to argue more. Their voices rose, and Napoleon suddenly threw himself back down into the bathtub. A wave of perfumed bath water left Joseph dripping from head to foot. Then the Emperor calmly got out of the tub and let a servant dry him off.

For Napoleon, Louisiana was to have been his steppingstone to conquering the Western Hemisphere. The Emperor intended to rule the world. He had sent his troops to take possession of the territory, but on their way, they were to stop by the French Caribbean

46

Louisiana's swamp land

colony of St. Domingue. Over ten years earlier, the St. Domingue slaves had rebelled and were now ruling themselves. Napoleon's men were to reestablish control of the colony and then move on to New Orleans.

The French soldiers had arrived in the Caribbean, anticipating an easy victory. Instead, they were faced with residents determined to keep their freedom. Men and women, children and the elderly, fought a ***guerrilla-style*** war against the French, ambushing them unexpectedly at every opportunity. In less than seven months, the French troops had been reduced from over 28,000 men to only 4,000. Despite re-

47

inforcements, attacks and yellow fever continued to eat away at French forces. Before long, they were forced to abandon the colony and St. Domingue became an independent nation, now known as Haiti.

As a result, Napoleon was having second thoughts about Louisiana. His losses in St. Domingue had cost him both money and men. He was facing a possible war with England that would also be very expensive. On top of this, the

Americans were protesting heatedly the French takeover of Louisiana. At this point, Napoleon could not afford to fight a war with the Americans, too.

When Thomas Jefferson became President of the United States in 1801, he began hearing rumors of the secret treaty between Spain and France. The idea of such a treaty worried Jefferson. If it were true that Napoleon had taken ownership of Louisiana, Jefferson anticipated war with France would not be long in coming.

The port of New Orleans

The Treaty of San Ildefonso

Although Spain's King, Charles IV, did not care about politics, his wife, Queen Maria Luisa did. In 1800, when Napoleon approached her and offered to buy the Louisiana Territory in exchange for part of Tuscany in Italy, she was interested and excited. Spain felt their North American land was worthless, taking money and men to govern and bringing nothing in return.

In the treaty, Napoleon promised to create the Kingdom of Etruria in Tuscany, where Maria Luisa's daughter Luisetta and her son-in-law Luis would rule. The treaty was kept a secret so America and Britain would not discover France now owned Louisiana. Napoleon also promised never to sell or give away any part of the North American territory unless it was to Spain.

Excited, Luisetta and Luis traveled to Etruria to begin ruling. They were shocked to discover their "kingdom" was actually still under Napoleon's control. French troops patrolled the area, and the true rulers were the French governors. A palace existed, but it was unfurnished and nearly a ruin. The couple moved into their new home, furnishing it with donations from kind local families, but they were mortified at the trick Napoleon had played on them.

Basically, Napoleon managed to get the huge Louisiana Territory from Spain for free. He allowed Luis and Luisetta to become the king and queen of Etruria, but they ruled in name only. Having gotten what he wanted, Napoleon then ignored his side of the treaty. Spain never owned Etruria, and in 1803 Napoleon sold Louisiana to the United States, breaking another part of his agreement with Spain.

Under Spanish control, Americans had gained the right to use the Mississippi River for shipping and to store goods in the warehouses of New Orleans at the mouth of the river. There was no guarantee these rights would exist in a French-ruled Louisiana.

*To **secede** means to withdraw from an organization.*

Seeking to avoid war with Napoleon, Jefferson took action. In October of 1801, Robert Livingston sailed from New York to become the new minister to France. Livingston's job was to try to convince the French not to take possession of Louisiana.

Livingston was frustrated with the task Jefferson had given him. Napoleon's ministers and advisors seemed incapable of influencing the Emperor. Napoleon made all the decisions himself, and a man such as Livingston was not often enough in the Emperor's presence to have any hope of influencing him directly. Complicating matters, Charles Maurice de Talleyrand, the French minister of foreign affairs, claimed repeatedly that France did not own Louisiana. Finally, months after his arrival in France, Livingston wrote to the American secretary of state, James Madison, confirming Napoleon planned to occupy Louisiana.

News that Napoleon had acquired Louisiana from the Spanish caused an uproar in the United States. People panicked and called for immediate war against France. Others threatened to **secede** from the Union and join whatever country held New Orleans.

Robert Livingston

While Jefferson tried to calm Americans' fears at home, Livingston continued to try and sway the French. He presented Napoleon's advisors with a long pamphlet called "Whether It Will Be Advantageous to France to Take Possession of Louisiana." The pamphlet suggested France should give New Orleans to the United

Talleyrand

Livingston. Monroe's instructions were to first offer to buy New Orleans and the land to the east of it for ten million dollars. If that failed, he was to offer to buy New Orleans alone. If Napoleon rejected that offer as well, Monroe was to demand that Americans be allowed to continue shipping on the Mississippi River and storing their goods in New Orleans. If all offers were rejected, Monroe would travel to England and negotiate an alliance.

James Monroe

States. America would make the port duty free to the French. Napoleon could use the city as much as he wanted without actually owning it. If France insisted on taking control of Louisiana, the pamphlet said, the United States would ally itself with England against France. Napoleon was not impressed with this threat.

Early in 1803, Jefferson sent James Monroe to Paris as an envoy extraordinary to join

The Transfer of New Orleans

News took so long to travel in the early 1800s that it was years before the people of Louisiana learned France now ruled them instead of Spain. In fact, by the time some learned of it, France had already sold Louisiana to the Americans.

Pierre Laussat was to be the French governor of Louisiana. He arrived in New Orleans in 1803 and spent months getting ready to begin his job. The thought of living in New Orleans as governor thrilled Laussat. His wife and daughters would arrive from France soon. He was enjoying himself.

On November 30, 1803, the Spanish flag was taken down and the French flag raised. Laussat was now governor. Then, twenty days later, on December 20, another transfer ceremony took place. The United States took possession of Louisiana, raising the American flag with a twenty-gun salute.

Laussat stood on the balcony of the Hôtel de Ville, tears streaming down his face as he gave control of the city to the Americans. His dream of being governor was over.

On April 11, 1803, the day before Monroe arrived in Paris, Livingston met with Talleyrand again. They had met together many times, and each time Talleyrand had brushed aside Livingston's talk of New Orleans and the Louisiana Territory. This time, however, the French minister abruptly asked the American how much the United States was willing to pay for Louisiana. Livingston was speechless. After a moment, he answered that the United States was not interested in all of Louisiana, just New Orleans.

When Monroe arrived in Paris, Livingston talked to him about the offer. French officials warned the Americans not to wait too long in deciding what to do. War was coming between France and England, they said, and when that happened, the English would attack New Orleans if it were still under French ownership.

*A flatboat on the Mississippi. The river
was an important transportation route
that flowed through New Orleans.*

Livingston and Monroe could not consult President Jefferson about the offer. In those days, letters took months to cross the Atlantic Ocean on slow-moving boats. The two Americans had no time to write to the President and wait for his response; they were on their own. Even though they knew they really had no authority to make such an enormous decision, they felt they had no choice.

Napoleon's first price for the North American territory was 22.5 million dollars. Livingston and Monroe offered to pay 8 million dollars. Over the next several weeks, the negotiations went back and forth. On April 30, a treaty was drawn up. The United States would pay 15 million dollars for the Louisiana Territory. They agreed to give France and Spain duty-free shipping out of New Orleans and other Louisiana ports.

The American diplomats did not, of course, have 15 million dollars in cash with them to pay for the land. The French minister of finance, Francois Barbé-Marbois, arranged for a British bank to lend the money to the United States. Before granting the loan, the bank consulted the British prime minister. The prime minister agreed to lend the money to the United States,

In Jefferson's day the land west of the Mississippi seemed so immense that Jefferson predicted it would take thousands of years to settle it all. He wrote that there was "land enough for our descendants to the thousandth and thousandth generation.

mostly because he wanted to make sure France was kept out of North America.

Initially, the United States thought France had also acquired Florida in their deal with Spain. Apart from the port of New Orleans, Jefferson wanted to make sure America could get control of Florida. Livingston and Monroe were disappointed to discover Spain still owned Florida. Eager to finish the Louisiana deal, the French promised to try and convince Spain to eventually sell to the United States.

On July 3, 1803, Jefferson got the news that Livingston and Monroe had purchased the entire Louisiana Territory—over 800,000 square miles. Suddenly, the area of the United States had doubled.

Livingston and Monroe must have wondered what Jefferson's reaction would be to the news. They had made an unauthorized—and large—purchase, and they had put the United States 15 million dollars in debt to do so. Any fears they might have had were groundless, however; Jefferson was thrilled. He had long dreamed of expanding westward. The new territory, with the fertile Mississippi, would become an immense "valley of democracy" for American settlers.

Before the Louisiana Purchase became official, Congress needed to approve it. Jefferson was concerned he had no legal right to authorize the purchase himself. He had always insisted on a strict interpretation of the Constitution, but the Constitution did not mention acquiring new

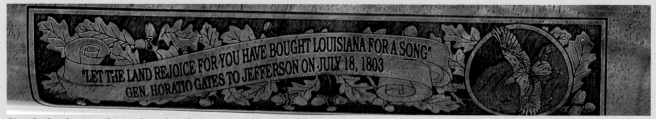

"Let the land rejoice for you have bought Louisiana for a song" (inscription on a gunstock given to Jefferson)

The transfer of Louisiana to the United States

land. Jefferson drafted a constitutional amendment that would make Louisiana part of the United States. This way, there could be no question about the constitutionality of the purchase.

An amendment would take time, however. In August, Jefferson received a letter from Livingston warning that Napoleon was considering backing out of the agreement. There was no longer any time to wait for the Constitution to be amended; Jefferson had to act as soon as possible.

Suppressing his concerns about strictly following the Constitution, Jefferson met with Congress and urged them to act quickly, debating the issue as little as possible. On October 20, 1803, the Senate approved the Louisiana Purchase Treaty by a vote of 24 to 7. On December 20, 1803, the United States took control of New Orleans and the Louisiana Territory. Neither the French nor the Americans ever considered that the land might belong to the people who already inhabited it—the various Native tribes who had lived there for centuries before the coming of white people.

Indian Presents

12 Pipe Tomahawks

6 ½ in: Steel Hut Iron

1 pieced flannel 47½ yds

11 p³ Handkerchiefs ass⁰

1 doz Ivory Combs

½ Catty Ind⁰ Silk

21 ℔ Seed ass⁰

1 p³ Scarlet Cloth 22½

3½ doz fan: Floss

6 Gro: Binding

2 Card Beads

4 doz: Butchers Knives

12 deg Pocket Looking Glasses d⁰ d⁰

15 doz Pewter d⁰ d⁰ d⁰

8 deg Nonsopretty

2 dog: Red Striped lapes

2 dg: Striped Silk Ribbon

72 p¹ Beads

3 ℔ Beads

6 papers Small Bells

1 box with 100 large d⁰

73 Bunches Beads ass⁰ ass⁰

3½ doz: Tinsil Bands ass⁰

A list of the items Lewis and Clark brought on their journey as gifts for the Natives they encountered

Four
THE LEWIS AND CLARK EXPEDITION: WESTWARD EXPANSION

In the distance, the peaks of snowcapped mountains sparkled in the early-morning sun. Captain William Clark stood on a hilltop and gazed across open land at his first glimpse of the Rocky Mountains. It was May 26, 1805. A year earlier, Clark had set out from St. Louis, Missouri, with his friend and co-captain, Meriwether Lewis, on an expedition across the continent of North America. They were to gather information about Indian tribes they met along the way, study the plants and wildlife of the West, learn the geography and make maps, and, especially, try to discover a water route to the Pacific that could be used for trade.

The explorers had expected they could follow the rivers, one after another, until at last they came to the Pacific Ocean. Now, here was a towering mountain range they would have to cross on foot. Reflecting on the sight, Clark optimistically wrote in his journal that night:

Whilst I viewed those mountains, I felt a secret pleasure in finding myself so near the head of the—heretofore

59

Anthropology is the study of human beings in relation to distribution, origin, classification, and relationship of races, physical character, environmental and social relations, and culture.

conceived—boundless Missouri [River]. But when I reflected on the difficulties which this snowy barrier would most probably throw in my way to the Pacific Ocean, and the sufferings and hardships of myself and party in them, it in some measure counterbalanced the joy I had felt in the first moments in which I gazed on them. But, as I have always held it little short of criminality to anticipate evils, I will allow it to be a good, comfortable road until I am compelled to believe otherwise.

On January 18, 1803, Thomas Jefferson sent a secret message to Congress proposing a "voyage of discovery" to explore the western part of the continent and seek out a trade route to the Pacific. The expedition would consist of "an intelligent officer, with ten or twelve chosen men." Jefferson asked Congress for only $2,500 to fund the voyage.

The intelligent officer Jefferson chose to lead the group was Meriwether Lewis, his twenty-eight-year-old personal secretary. To prepare him, Jefferson sent Lewis to Philadelphia for a crash course in science, medicine, and *anthropology*. The professors at the University of Pennsylvania taught him how to preserve plants, how to navigate by the stars, how to deal with medical problems he would probably encounter, and what questions to ask the Indians to learn about their society. Lewis also spent the $2,500 Congress had allowed him and bought nearly two tons of supplies for the trip; included among the supplies were gifts for the Indians, such as ribbons, tobacco, knives, and beads.

In June 1803, Lewis wrote to his friend and former commanding officer, William Clark, asking him to join him as co-captain on the

Meriwether Lewis

William Clark (left), Thomas Jefferson (center), and Meriwether Lewis (right)

expedition. Clark agreed, and Lewis then chose the other men to accompany them, looking for those skilled in hunting, interpreting, or frontier survival.

Most of the preparations were done in secret. Jefferson told the press Lewis would be explor-ing the area around the Mississippi. The United States did not own the land the Corps of Discovery would travel through. Some of the continent was owned by the Spanish, some by the French (at least until the Louisiana Purchase was finalized), and some by the

British. The Russians had recently colonized Alaska. Most of these countries were eager to expand their own possessions in North America and would not be happy to realize the United States was thinking about doing the same thing.

When news of the Louisiana Purchase reached Jefferson, the main reason for secrecy disappeared. The expedition would have had to cross into foreign territory as soon as they started out. Now they could travel freely across America's own land.

Jefferson gave Lewis detailed instructions about his mission. Lewis's main object was to find a trade route, but after that he was also to make precise notes about everything he discovered: the shape of the land, the animals that lived there—especially those not found in the eastern part of the continent—and the climate. Jefferson was particularly interested in the western Indian tribes. Lewis was to assure all Indians he met that the United States wanted to live in peace and friendship with them. The government would pay the traveling expenses of any chief who wished to visit Washington. If the Indians decided they wanted some of their children educated in American schools, the government would take care of that, too.

Lewis and Clark's journals

Lewis and Clark talking with Indians they met on their journey

Jefferson's Instructions to Meriwether Lewis

President Jefferson wrote a long letter to Lewis on June 20, 1803, giving him instructions for his journey.

Your observations are to be taken with great pains and accuracy; to be entered distinctly and intelligibly for others as well as yourself; to comprehend all the elements necessary, with the aid of the usual tables, to fix the latitude and longitude of the places at which they were taken. . . .

The commerce which may be carried on with the people inhabiting the line you will pursue, renders a knowledge of those people important. You will therefore endeavor to make yourself acquainted, as far as a diligent pursuit of your journey shall admit, with the names of the nations and their numbers;

The extent and limits of their possessions;

Their relations with other tribes or nations;

Their language, traditions, monuments;

Their ordinary occupations in agriculture, fishing, hunting, war, arts, and the implements for these;

Their food, clothing, and domestic accommodations;

The diseases prevalent among them, and the remedies they use;

Moral and physical circumstances which distinguish them from the tribes we know;

Peculiarities in their laws, customs, and dispositions;

And articles of commerce they may need or furnish, and to what extent. . . .

Other objects worthy of notice will be;

The soil and face of the country, its growth and vegetable productions, especially those not of the United States;

The animals of the country generally, and especially those not known in the United States;

The remains and accounts of any which may be deemed rare or extinct;

The mineral productions of every kind, but more particularly metals, lime-stone, pit-coal, and saltpeter; saline's and mineral waters, noting the temperature of the last, and such circumstances as may indicate their character;

Volcanic appearances;

Climate, as characterized by the thermometer, by the proportion of rainy, cloudy, and clear days; by lightning, hail, snow, ice; by the access and recess of frost; by the winds prevailing at different seasons; the dates at which particular plants put forth, or lose their flower or leaf; times of appearance of particular birds, reptiles or insects.

A drawing of one of the wildlife specimens brought back by Lewis and Clark

The Lewis and Clark expedition took nearly two and a half years to complete its mission. Most of the time—eighteen months—was spent on the voyage west. Although Jefferson's goal of finding a water route across the continent was not fulfilled, the journey was a success. Lewis and Clark were not the first white men to travel

While Lewis extended the goodwill of the U.S. government to the Indians of the West, he was to study them. Jefferson wanted his secretary to bring back information on the languages, culture, and land holdings of the Indians he met, as well as their relations with other tribes and the potential for trade with them.

On May 14, 1804, Jefferson's Corps of Discovery left their winter camp on the east side of the Mississippi and set out on the Missouri River. People lined the banks to watch them go, waving as their boats passed. The voyage of discovery had begun.

The Flatheads were one of the tribes Lewis and Clark encountered

across North America, but they were probably the best organized. They brought back accounts of the Indians they encountered: their clothing, customs, and lists of vocabulary from their languages. Lewis and Clark also described 122 new animals and 178 new plants.

The biggest result of the Lewis and Clark expedition was the opening up of the West to settlers. Before Jefferson's Corps of Discovery returned with their volumes of notes, people did not know what kind of mysterious creatures lived on the western half of North America.

Sacajawea

Sacajawea has become famous as the guide of the Lewis and Clark expedition, leading the explorers across the wilderness with her baby boy strapped to her back. At the time of the expedition, she was about seventeen years old. She was a Shoshone Indian who had been kidnapped by another tribe five years earlier.

Sacajawea was one of the wives of Toussaint Charbonneau, a fur trader. When Lewis and Clark hired Charbonneau to guide them, he took Sacajawea with him because she could speak a number of Indian languages.

Charbonneau turned out not to be an outstanding guide; several times he panicked when wind shook the boat he was steering. During one incident, he became so upset the boat overturned, spilling supplies and papers into the river. Fortunately, Sacajawea was able to save most of the cargo.

Today, Sacajawea is almost more famous than Lewis and Clark themselves. There are twenty-three statues of her in America—more than of any other woman. She was a woman and a Native American at a time when both those things were thought to make her inferior. Instead, she became an invaluable member of the Corps of Discovery, respected by the men with whom she traveled.

Lewis and Clark explored the rivers that ran into the Mississippi.

Covered wagon

part of the continent became simply an extension of the country with which Americans were familiar.

Jefferson died before the wagon trains started rolling across the Oregon Trail to the Pacific, but in his lifetime he saw the spread of settlers into the Louisiana Territory. As towns and cities grew up in the new territory, the people began to form states. With new states joining the country, however, the issue of slavery became very important. Would the new states be slave or free?

Article III of the Louisiana Purchase said the residents of the Louisiana Territory were to be "protected in the free enjoyment of their liberty, property and the religion which they profess." Since slaves were considered property, and slavery already existed in the new territory, most people believed the purchase treaty now protected the institution of slavery.

In 1805 and 1806, Congress fiercely debated the problem of slavery and the new territory. Northern anti-slavery supporters fought to outlaw the transportation of slaves into the Louisiana Territory. Southern congressmen argued that without slavery, Louisiana's economy would shrivel and die. Slaves, they claimed, were needed to work the farms. It was too hot

Jefferson himself believed the explorers would probably run into giant sloths, wooly mammoths, and other prehistoric creatures. Some of the men thought a race of cruel giants lived in the West.

As more and more people traveled west and returned with descriptions of what they had found, the West stopped looking like such a strange and exotic place. Gradually, the western

Slaves working with cotton gin

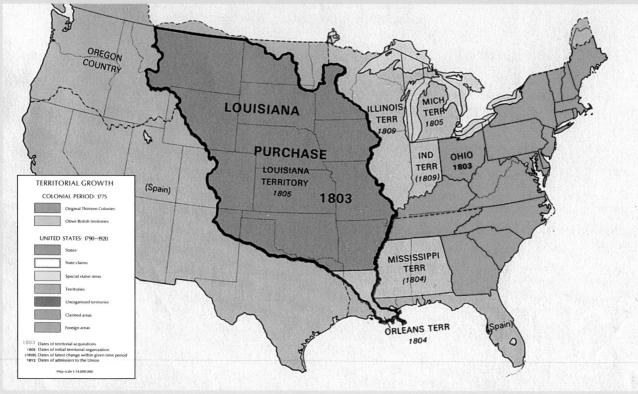

Map of territorial growth, 1810

for white men to work in such a place; only the black slaves could survive to do the labor needed.

Despite the efforts of the anti-slavery proponents, the slave trade continued throughout the southern part of the Louisiana Territory. In 1793, Eli Whitney had developed a cotton gin, simplifying the processing of cotton. Before this, slavery was mostly contained in the Southern coastal states. The number of slaves was not increasing greatly, since people had as many slaves as they could use. With the introduction of cotton as a profitable crop, however, suddenly everybody wanted more slaves and more land. Plantations sprang up across the South, bringing the slavery system with them.

The development of the Southern "cotton culture" inspired more inventors to build machines to support the cotton industry. Machines to spin and weave cotton were invented, and the steamship made transporting the crops easier. A better understanding of agriculture led to the introduction of improved farming techniques such as ***crop rotation***, making the industry more productive. All these advances strengthened the hold of cotton in the South and by doing so strengthened the hold of slavery.

Again, despite Jefferson's claim that he hated slavery, he did nothing to hinder its spread. He believed Article III of the Louisiana Purchase Treaty granted slave owners the right to continue owning and trading their slaves. He thought perhaps an expansion of slavery was just what was needed to bring an end to the terrible injustice being done to African Americans. Toward the end of his life, he wrote:

> We feel and deplore it [slavery] morally and politically, and we look without entire despair to some redeeming means not yet specifically foreseen. I am happy in believing that the conviction of the necessity of removing this evil gains ground with time. Their emigration to the westward lightens the difficulty by dividing it, and renders it more practicable on the whole.

Through his purchase of the Louisiana Territory and his organization of the Lewis and Clark expedition across the continent, Jefferson helped to open up the West to settlers. As the population moved west, so did slavery, but Jefferson believed it would not last forever. He foresaw a time when slavery would end, although he feared it would take a war to do it. He was right, of course.

Crop rotation is the farming practice of alternating the types of crops planted on the land to keep the soil from losing its nutrients.

Cotton

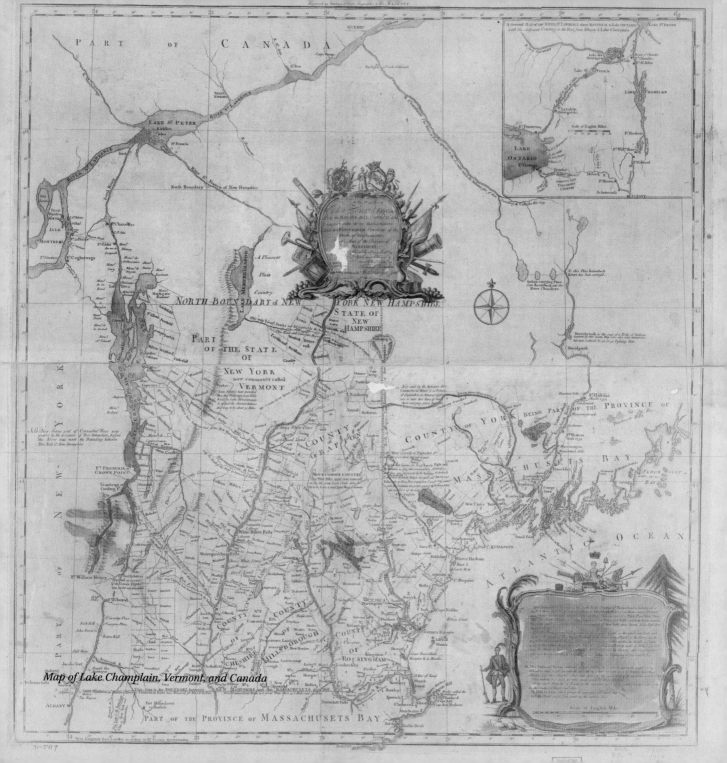

Map of Lake Champlain, Vermont, and Canada

Five
THE DOWNFALL OF NEUTRAL AMERICA

On a moonless night in the winter of 1808, a horse-drawn sled glided quietly across the ice at the northern end of Lake Champlain. The dark bulk of the sled, piled high with large bundles, could be seen dimly against the lighter snow on the frozen lake. A man sat on the driver's seat of the sled, his shoulders hunched against the cold. As the sled rounded a point of land, the man reined in the horse and stared hard at the shoreline ahead. After a moment, he clucked softly and the sled started moving again.

He had gone no more than several hundred feet when there was a sudden shout from among the trees in front of him. He cursed under his breath and yanked hard on the reins, pulling the horse away from the shore and steering toward the far bank.

"Stop now, or I'll shoot!" the army man yelled. The sled sped on across the ice. A moment later, a gunshot echoed across the lake. A bullet grazed the wood of the sled, but the driver paid no attention. The men behind him were on foot, and their shouts receded into the dark night as the horse raced across the frozen lake, carrying the sled and its cargo to safety.

He had eluded the army patrols, but it was another three hours before the man with the

*A **rendezvous** is a meeting.*

***Contraband** is an illegal or prohibited good.*

sled made his ***rendezvous*** near the village of Alburg. He was nearly an hour late, but he had escaped once again with his load of ***contraband***. The bolts of cloth, barrels of rum, and packages of tea, sugar, and tobacco he carried would fetch a good price in Albany, and the money would help feed his family for another month.

Trade was the lifeblood of the economy along the border between British Canada and the United States. Most of the people of

Napoleon on board one of his battleships

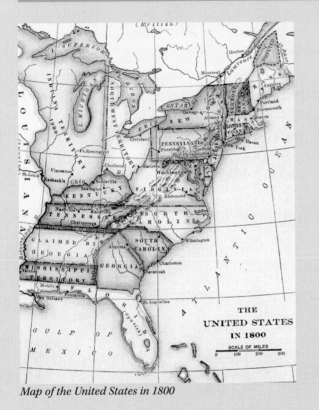

Map of the United States in 1800

Unfortunately, relations were not good between the United States and Europe. Europe was in the middle of the Napoleonic Wars, struggling to keep the French emperor from taking over all the lands around him. By 1807, Napoleon had conquered much of Western Europe and was mainly battling England. The United States, who did business with both countries, tried hard to stay neutral.

Neutrality was not easy for the United States. America had been struggling with the issue ever since the Napoleonic Wars had begun in 1793. The same year war broke out in Europe, George Washington had issued the Proclamation of Neutrality, stating America should "with sincerity and good faith adopt and pursue a conduct

northern Vermont and New York did not care what the relationship was between their country and Britain, as long as goods were allowed to keep flowing back and forth across the border. Even when the government outlawed trade, many continued carrying goods across the border. Scenes like the one just described happened countless times.

Napoleonic Wars

friendly and impartial toward the belligerent Powers."

Over the next decade, as the fighting stopped and started in Europe, Americans lived their own lives and focused on their own new country. There were periods of peace in Europe—the negotiation of the Louisiana Purchase hap-

pened during one of these—but as long as Napoleon stayed in power, war was never far away. Napoleon refused to be satisfied while England remained free; in fact, he wanted to eventually rule the whole world.

The United States unwillingly became involved in the European conflict as both Britain

A battle at sea

and France refused to respect the U.S. neutrality policy. Britain and France were nearly equally matched, but they had very different strengths; Britain had an almost unbeatable navy, while France's army ruled on land. To make up for their lack of naval strength, France captured American merchant ships. Napoleon claimed any

Conscripting means drafting into military service.

Emigrants are people who have left one country to settle in another.

foreign ships entering British ports were effectively British ships, and therefore France had the right to seize them.

Britain's policies were not any easier on the Americans. The British began forcibly *conscripting* people to serve in their navy, a process called impressment. "Press gangs" walked the streets of British cities, looking for former sailors to kidnap and "press" into service. When British ships encountered American ships on the ocean, they boarded them and looked for British citizens to take for their navy. They ignored the fact most of these men were *emigrants* who had left Britain and become American citizens. Six

The press gang

By the Commissioners for Executing the Office of Lord High Admiral of the United Kingdom of Great Britain and Ireland, &c. and of all His Majesty's Plantations, &c.

IN PURSUANCE OF HIS MAJESTY'S ORDER in Council, dated the Sixteenth Day of November, 1804, We do hereby Impower and Direct you to impress, or cause to be impressed, so many Seamen, Seafaring Men and Persons whose Occupations and Callings are to work in Vessels and Boats upon Rivers, as shall be necessary either to Man His Majesty's Ships, giving unto each Man so impressed One Shilling for Prest Money. And in the execution hereof, you are to take care that neither yourself nor any Officer authorized by you do demand or receive any Money, Gratuity, Reward or other Consideration whatsoever, for the sparing, Exchanging, or Discharging, any Person or Persons impressed or to be impressed as you will answer to it at your Peril. You are not to intrust any Person with the execution of this Warrant, but a Commission Officer and to insert his Name and Office in the Deputation on the other side hereof, and set you Hand and Seal thereto.—This Warrant to continue in Force till the Thirty First Day of December 1809, and in the due execution thereof, all Mayors, Sheriffs, Justices of the Peace, Baliffs, Constables Headboroughs, and all the His Majesty's Officers and Subjects whom it may concern, are hereby required to be aiding and assisting unto you, and those employed by you, as they tender His Majesty's Service, and will answer the contrary at their Perils.

Given under the Hand and the Seal of the Office of the Admiralty, 1809.

Captain
Commander of His Majesty's Navy
By Command of Their Lordships.

Impressment warrant issued by the English king

President Jefferson distrusted a strong military and had cut back the American army and navy. He felt a powerful fighting force could too easily be used to oppress the people. He only needed to look at Europe and see what Napoleon had done with the French army to see the dangers.

The American Navy at this time mainly consisted of a fleet of small gunboats used to patrol

Thomas Jefferson

thousand men were taken from American ships through British impressment, most of them citizens of the United States.

The American people were furious at the way France and Britain were treating them. Some Americans clamored for war, but the United States was not prepared to fight a war.

U.S. gunboats

*An **embargo** is a government prohibition on the departure of ships from its ports.*

the harbors. These gunboats were only useful for defense and were not meant to be taken far from shore.

Jefferson wanted to keep the American policy of neutrality, but he knew he could not let the situation with Europe continue. Instead of war, he proposed a trade **embargo**, restricting trade with the warring European countries. The embargo was supposed to make Europe realize how much it depended on the United States for shipments of things such as cotton, tobacco, and grain. In 1807, Congress passed the Embargo Act.

The Embargo Act was not the success Jefferson had hoped. The embargo did not bother Europe; they had plenty of American goods piled in their warehouses and it would be several years before they felt the shortage.

Thomas Jefferson

Instead of hurting Europe, the embargo actually ended up hurting the United States. Merchants and ship owners lost money without goods to transport and sell. New England factories that relied on European goods for parts went out of business. Cotton and tobacco stores overflowed the barns of the South.

The American people were angry. Parts of New England even threatened to leave the Union. They had wanted President Jefferson to do something about their problems with Europe, but this was not what they had in mind. People along the borders took up smuggling, ignoring the embargo. Smuggling in northern Vermont and the Lake Champlain area was especially common. Men drove herds of cows through the passes of the Green Mountains. On the lake, they took boats laden with goods north to Canada, returning fully loaded with British merchandise.

Jefferson had hoped to help the United States by restricting trade with Europe. Instead, he found himself going against the principles of individual freedoms he believed in. He did not believe an army should be used against its own people, but he declared the Lake Champlain area in rebellion and sent in the Army to control the smuggling. More often than not, though, the

Tobacco stores overflowed Southern barns.

smugglers were able to evade the patrols. Trade continued across the border with Canada as it had before the Embargo Act.

Finally giving in to the demands of the American people, Jefferson lifted the embargo three days before he left office as President, allowing trade with all European countries except France and Britain. The next year, his successor,

James Madison, lifted this restriction as well.

Although it infuriated the American people and was considered a failure in its time, the Embargo Act did have at least one lasting positive effect. Without needed goods arriving regularly from Europe, America was at a loss. Not able to rely on Europe, the United States found ways to look after itself. To make up for the shortages, factories began opening up in the North. The ***industrialism*** of the Northeast was strengthened during this time.

The American people continue to be fascinated by Thomas Jefferson, even two hundred years after he left office. In 2002 alone—the 250th anniversary of Jefferson's birth—nearly fifty books were published with his name in the title. Jefferson was a philosopher, a farmer, a musician, an inventor, a diplomat, and an architect, not to mention the author of the Declaration of

Industrialism *is the social organization in which large-scale industries are allowed to flourish.*

A northeastern factory

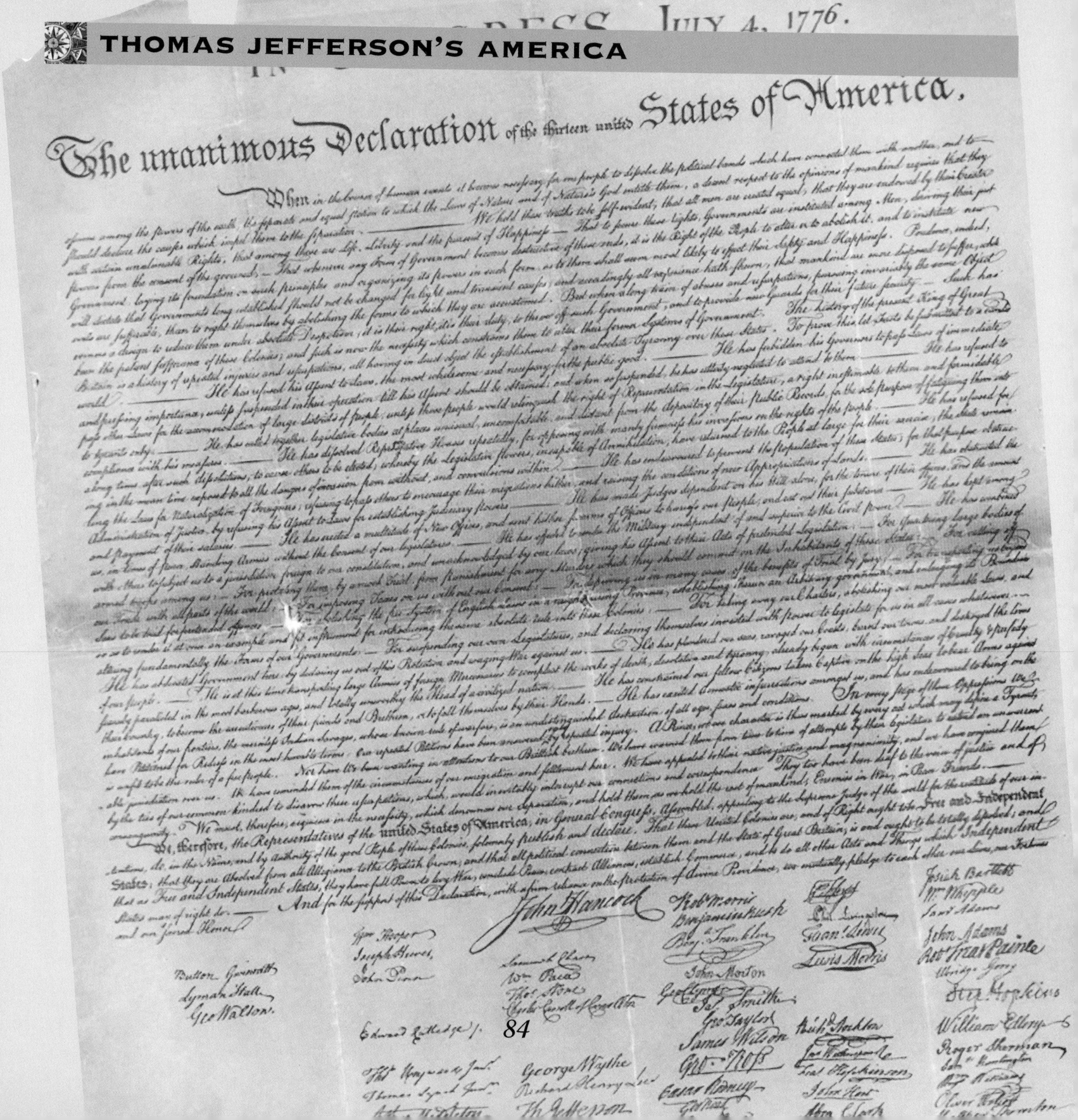
JULY 4, 1776.
The unanimous Declaration of the thirteen united States of America,

Independence and the third President of the United States.

Over the past thirty-five years or so, some historians have started to question Jefferson's character. He claimed to hate slavery, but he owned hundreds of slaves. He claimed to love the Indians, but he drove them from their homes. Scholars questioned what these things said about Jefferson's integrity. A few historians even said Americans should stop honoring Jefferson altogether.

In spite of the scholars' attacks, many Americans still like and respect Jefferson. Most people have never read the articles criticizing Jefferson's character, but they have read the Declaration of Independence. The words of the Declaration still thrill us: We hold these truths to be self-evident, that all men are created equal, that they are endowed by their Creator with certain unalienable Rights, that among these are Life, Liberty and the pursuit of Happiness.

Every day, modern politicians—Democrats, Republicans, and Independents—quote Jefferson's words in speeches. Newspapers compare current leaders with Jefferson. Jefferson believed in individual freedoms: the freedom of speech, the freedom of religion, the freedom of the press.

Thomas Jefferson

Jefferson was not a twenty-first-century man, but many of the values he held two centuries ago are still cherished by Americans today. We may be uncomfortable with parts of his life— such as his slave ownership—but the strength of his vision for the United States, his insistence that freedom for all people was a right, still inspires us hundreds of years after his death. Jefferson, along with the other Founding Fathers of our country, has left us with the unshakable belief that "Life, Liberty, and the pursuit of Happiness" are our rights as Americans.

THOMAS JEFFERSON'S AMERICA

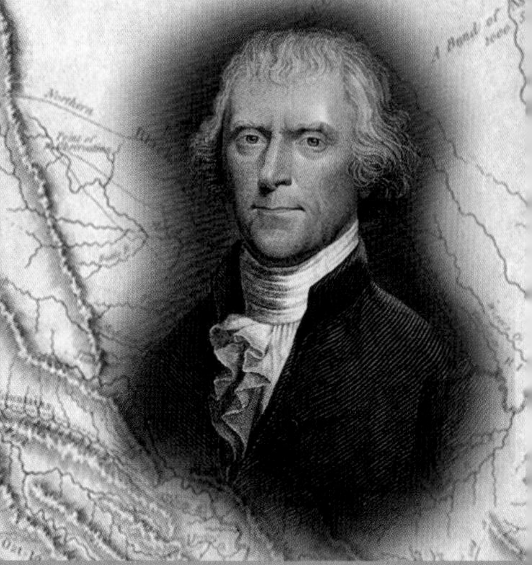

April 13, 1743 Thomas Jefferson is born at Shadwell plantation in Virginia.

June–July 1776 As a delegate to the Second Continental Congress, Jefferson writes the Declaration of Independence.

1793 Eli Whitney develops the cotton gin.

1796 Thomas Jefferson runs for President against John Adams. When Jefferson loses to Adams he becomes Adams' Vice President.

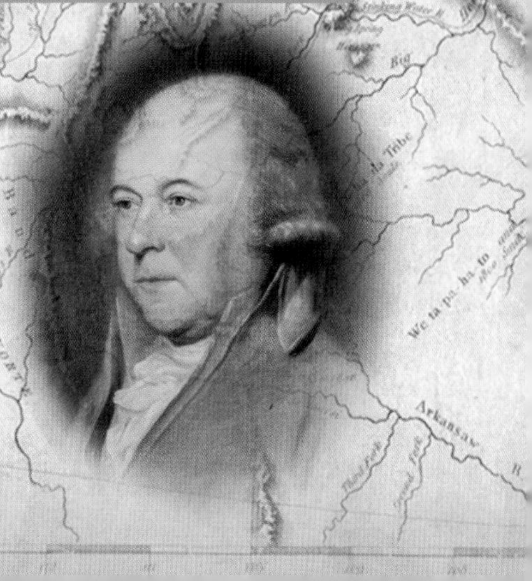

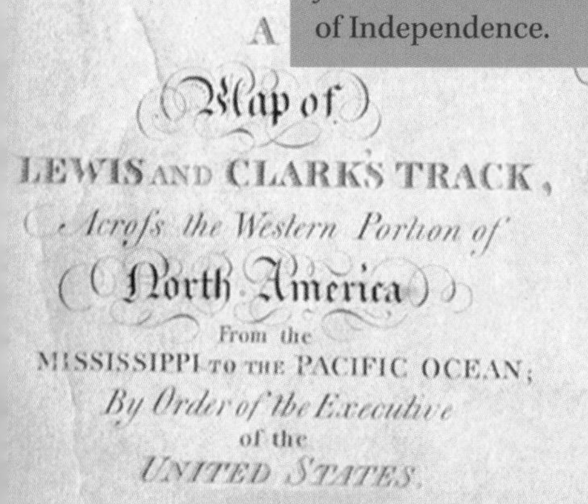

A
Map of
LEWIS AND CLARK'S TRACK,
Across the Western Portion of
North America
From the
MISSISSIPPI TO THE PACIFIC OCEAN;
By Order of the Executive
of the
UNITED STATES.

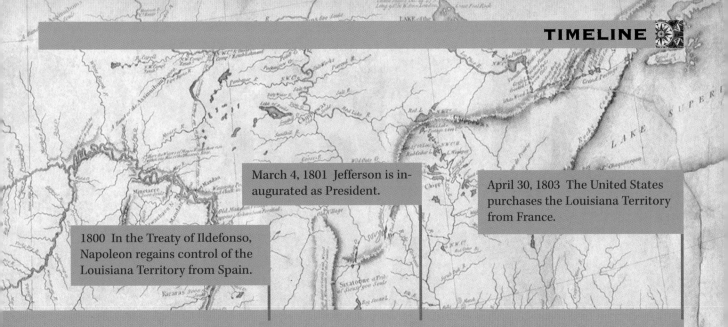

March 4, 1801 Jefferson is in-augurated as President.

April 30, 1803 The United States purchases the Louisiana Territory from France.

1800 In the Treaty of Ildefonso, Napoleon regains control of the Louisiana Territory from Spain.

1800 Jefferson runs for President against Adams again. This time Jefferson is elected President.

January 1, 1802 Jefferson writes a letter to the Baptist Association of Danbury, Connecticut, assuring them of their religious freedom. From this letter came the phrase, "the separation of church and state."

1798 Congress passes the Alien and Sedition Acts, raising the residency requirement for citizenship from five to fourteen years, giving the President the power to deport any for-eigner he thought could be dangerous, and making it a crime to publish false, negative information about the President or other gov-ernment figures.

1804 Jefferson is reelected President.

1803–1815 Napoleonic Wars. Napoleon fights a series of wars against the nations of Europe. Although the United States is neutral in the conflicts, both France and England continue attacking American ships. In 1807, Congress responds by passing the Embargo Act.

September 1806 Lewis and Clark's Corps of Discovery returns.

December 20, 1803 Transfer ceremony in New Orleans. The French flag is lowered and the American flag is raised.

November 7, 1805 The Lewis and Clark expedition reaches the Pacific Ocean.

May 14, 1804 Meriwether Lewis and William Clark leave from Missouri on their Voyage of Discovery to the Pacific Ocean.

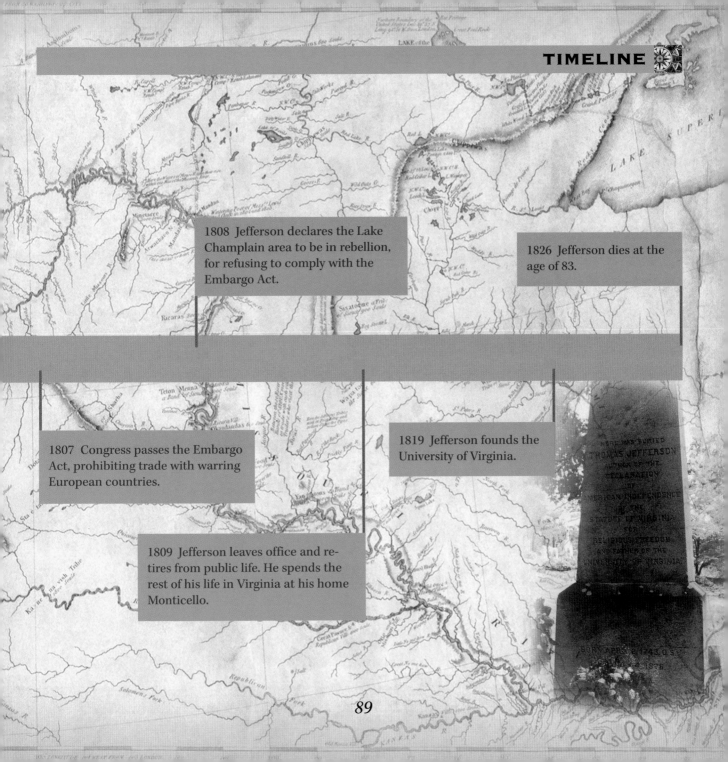

1808 Jefferson declares the Lake Champlain area to be in rebellion, for refusing to comply with the Embargo Act.

1826 Jefferson dies at the age of 83.

1807 Congress passes the Embargo Act, prohibiting trade with warring European countries.

1819 Jefferson founds the University of Virginia.

1809 Jefferson leaves office and retires from public life. He spends the rest of his life in Virginia at his home Monticello.

FURTHER READING

Blumberg, Rhoda. *The Incredible Journey of Lewis and Clark.* New York: Beech Tree, 1997.

Blumberg, Rhoda. *What's the Deal? Jefferson, Napoleon, and the Louisiana Purchase.* Washington, D.C.: National Geographic Society, 1998.

Chase, John. *Louisiana Purchase: An American Story.* Gretna, La.: Pelican Publishing Company, 2002.

Nardo, Don. *The Declaration of Independence: A Model for Individual Rights.* San Diego: Lucent, 1999.

Phelan, Mary Kay. *The Story of the Louisiana Purchase.* New York: Thomas Y. Crowell, 1979.

Reef, Catherine. *Monticello.* New York: Dillon, 1991.

Rowland, Della. *The Story of Sacajawea: Guide to Lewis and Clark.* New York: Dell, 1989.

St. George, Judith. *Sacajawea.* New York: G. P. Putnam's Sons, 1997.

FOR MORE INFORMATION

Thomas Jefferson
www.americanpresident.org/history/
thomasjefferson

Jefferson's Writings
www.yale.edu/lawweb/avalon/presiden/
jeffpap

Jefferson's Life at Monticello
www.monticello.org

The Louisiana Purchase
www.jeffersonnapoleon.com/time

The Lewis and Clark Expedition
www.pbs.org/lewisandclark

Publisher's note:
The Web sites listed on this page were active at the time of publication. The publisher is not responsible for Web sites that have changed their addresses or discontinued operation since the date of publication. The publisher will review and update the Web sites upon each reprint.

INDEX

BIOGRAPHIES

AUTHOR

Sheila Nelson has always been fascinated with history and the lives of historical figures. She enjoys studying history and learning more about the events and people that have shaped our world. Sheila has written several books on history and other subjects. Recently, she completed a master's degree and now lives in Rochester, New York, with her husband and their baby daughter.

SERIES CONSULTANT

Dr. Jack N. Rakove is a professor of history and American studies at Stanford University, where he is director of American studies. The winner of the 1997 Pulitzer Prize in history, Dr. Rakove is the author of *The Unfinished Election of 2000, Constitutional Culture and Democratic Rule,* and *James Madison and the Creation of the American Republic.* He is also the president of the Society for the History of the Early American Republic.

PICTURE CREDITS

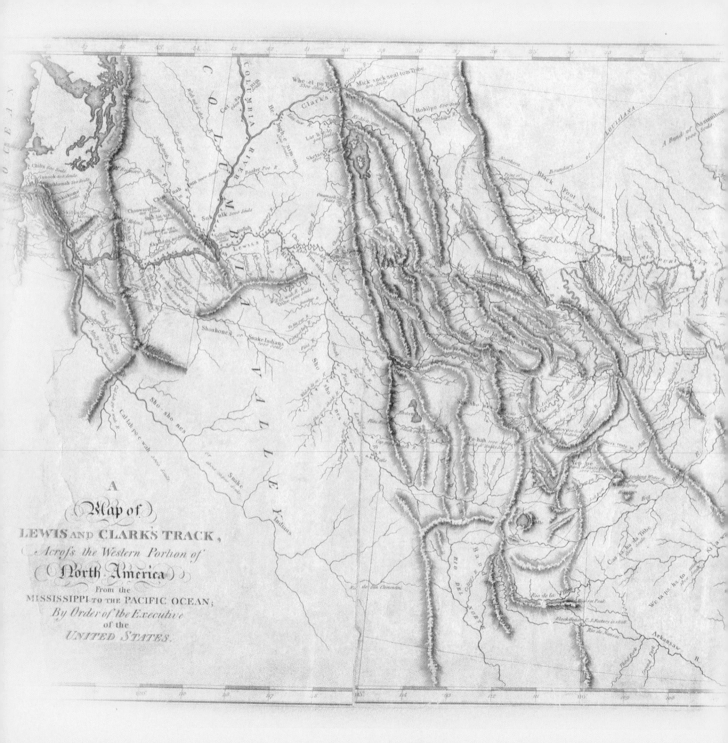

A
Map of
LEWIS AND CLARK'S TRACK,
Across the Western Portion of
North America
From the
MISSISSIPPI TO THE PACIFIC OCEAN;
By Order of the Executive
of the
UNITED STATES.